Stumble, Gorgeous

Paula McLain

New Issues Poetry & Prose

A Green Rose Book

New Issues Poetry & Prose
The College of Arts and Sciences
Western Michigan University
Kalamazoo, Michigan 49008

An Inland Seas Poetry Book

Inland Seas poetry books are supported by a grant from
The Michigan Council for Arts and Cultural Affairs.

First Edition, 2005.

ISBN   1-930974-56-6 (paperbound)

Library of Congress Cataloging-in-Publication Data:
McLain, Paula
Stumble, Gorgeous/Paula McLain
Library of Congress Control Number: 2005922614

Editor   Herbert Scott
Copy Editor   Lisa Lishman
Managing Editor   Marianne E. Swierenga
Designer   Joshua Levi
Art Director   Tricia Hennessy
Production Manager   Paul Sizer
                                The Design Center, Department of Art
                                College of Fine Arts
                                Western Michigan University

Stumble, Gorgeous

Paula McLain

New Issues

 WESTERN MICHIGAN UNIVERSITY

Also by Paula McLain

Less of Her

Like Family: Growing up in Other People's Houses, a memoir

for Greg

Contents

What a chimera, then, is man! What a novelty!
What a monster, what a chaos, what a contradiction,
what a prodigy! Judge of all things, imbecile worm of the earth;
depository of truth, a sink of uncertainty and error; the pride
and refuse of the universe!

—Blaise Pascal

I. Enough with the Angels

Our Father Who Art in Albuquerque

Or is it Duluth, now? Missoula?

Hallowed be your overalls,
Your stringer of fish,

The hummock where you stand,
Photographable, a pulled-taffy sunset

Held aloft by conifers and your unlikely
Shoulders.

Funny how a kingdom comes, jerry-built—
Slipshod—pocket wilderness

Squeezed into and worn until worn through.

Our Father, we say at parties, or don't say but telegraph
By listing toward plastic cups, married men,

(Those who trespass against us)—any groove
Grown impervious to earth

As it is to heaven. Give us this. *We are weak,
Father.* Forgive us this.

We learn to love by loving silhouette:
Whetstone: the squeak of wet bread

Gummed. We learn to love as a kind of jangling
Prayer, vernacular cant to the floppy horizon,

The unhearing, unheard from hole *at the center of.*
We the flock, I mean,

The forcefully lost, the daughters
On this twitching promenade.

When you get this, please don't answer.
Just blink once. Or shake the globe

And set us snowing. Or blow a cold
Unanswerable kiss.

Heaven

Some of it was like dying, and some of the dying
Was like myth: the afterlife predicted in tapestry
Or dog rose strangling stained glass.

In such light we lay down. Columbine and a bridle
Of damp rope. Butterflies lifting, prismed, pitiless.

In practical terms, we were children—mortal
And possessed. We folded easily into handbags and teacups,
Leaned into a father's mood. Nighttime

Became motif, patterns of shadow crippling the wall
Like two trolls tugging on one another's beards
Until they wore their skins on the inside,

Nothing touchable without. We were told early about the sky,
How beyond its crystal vault lived water. This was our blue—

Everything lovely and thunderous; every someday flood
Plaited with celestial fish, with seaweed radiant and constellated.
We dreamed it down again and again,

Held our breath, kicked into the mermaid firmament,
Wet glamour eroding our edges, grafting
Us to each other and the splendid millstone world.

Enough with the Angels

Ditto the sublime with bird-swamped dawn
And a plate of Bosc pears. The peacock can stay,
But why not a little less dazzle in the redemption scene?
A little more rent? Something with ass-kicking consequences?
Yesterday was closer to sandbag than key lime pie,
So let's give the shepherdess more to do, a chewed shoelace for a boa,
A Des Moines kind of longing. Yellow light and soul litter.

One night my sister came into my room and kissed me
Quietly on the forehead. *I'm so glad you're here,* she said. This was after
We'd stuttered our way through the wrecked nests and cul-de-sacs.
After seven-eighths of the damage and the commandeering of our several
    selves
To Ball jars in a fly-snagged hutch. After the sour facts but before I knew
I would ransom even her to save myself. That I would count my money
    running.

This is the way it goes for you and me. We have covered some ground.
Have hummed the night thicker. Have keened. Have sucker punched
The moon's clown face then set the break, kissed it, said
I'm so glad you're here. We are too tired, now, to talk back. To sass
Our stupid beginnings. Too tired to do anything but shove for space
Enough in the aisles to lie down. Rest our licorice eyes a while.

Something with a flatter heel is all I'm saying. A thinner lip.
Banana peel stand-in for the balcony scene. Kazoo for the aubade.
If we have to make due with angels, let there be less radiance waiting
In the folded wing. Less found.

Acrobats with Oranges

Above: canvas pulled into taffy. Below—
Smoke-white ponies, taffeta-collared bears,
Clowns and unicycles and cosmonauts
Trussed for the cannon.

My sister and I stand to one side and find
We're children again, but better at it now.
We've stopped tugging at our lisle stockings,
The rub of over-starched plackets, our place
In the Pleiades of the ring. We don't fidget.
We don't forget our names when the spots
Come up, bathing us blind.

We're given the same stakes nightly:
Six ripe oranges and gravity's carousel. We're given
Our dainty feet in Mary Janes, our manicured
Hands. We're given beauty we can block and closet
After hours, preserving its use.

At show time, we're something to see.
Our faces bud and blur behind quickened
Cargo. You might think *sleight of hand*
But it's closer to skywriting what we do. We spell a wheel,
An egg, a climbing compass. We spell the world
And it spells back everything it knows.

Above, the tightrope flosses forever. Below,
The lion tamer's grand mustache. Above,
Star-fizzle, startled moths, the asteroids of other lives
Careening. Below, air struck and plumbed,
Obvious with oranges.

Heaven

For years I lay in the switch grass, beetles
Like zebras in my safari. The thistle pod, the mica,
The flinch of small hairs—all of these were giants.

I was *more than*. I was an eye beaded and beset,
Harassed by the flammable yellows. What I was
To the manic bug world, heat was to me. Continental.

Planetary. Rivets of it slung up from the sulfur,
The asphalt, the average livid day like radio.
It was too much: I miss this. The way it pilfered.

The way it hammered holes in us and in the air.

A certain feel of the air is what's missing.
We were short on water, but tall on pricker weeds,
Tall on fence wire, tall on lack. A certain *lack*

Is part of what's missing. Relevant dent housed
Near the ribs: farmer-less dell. Imagine cupping
Your hands around a burning thing so it won't fizzle

Out. It sending sulfur through the fissures,
Sending yellow and a finger bone of heat. Imagine
Wanting to open your hands. Imagine resisting.

For years it was summer. Grasshoppers fluttered

And came unstuck with the *pop click* of a child's toy
Or the simplest of cameras. I wasn't dreaming.
There was a fig tree, a horse, a hollow space

Where we stopped to rest. Where we starved
And sucked our lips and considered the dotted-Swiss
Clouds, the everywhere sky. The sky is what's missing.

The way the sky *attended*. I wasn't dreaming, I was alive
In the yellow grass. A fuse, wick, girl-sized torch.

Old Testament

Behind the ordinary door of childhood—that purview,
That burning—I played. Like Shadrack
In my cotton shorts, my peevishness. Like Meshack

With my Barbies askew. We got on like a natural disaster.
Tea parties—the loaves and the fishes—fashion shows,
Sacrificial torching of up-dos.

Pillaged and rent, Skipper and Ken grew sentimental,
A soggy knot I could sell anything to. I wrote them duets
As it was in the garden, set the apple sparking

On string between them. Meanwhile the house had gone
Atomic—chimney seizing around its wick,
Staircase unladdered, assuming tallow. One sister

Stood alone in the orchard. Another treaded
The volcano's serrated lip. I stayed in my room,
Salting coils of smoke. My dolls ate while I fasted. I plotted

While they whined, warming their plastic hands
On the grate of me. Years passed: the same old Gomorrah.
The house was a kiln, blistered, fanatic.

The chimney seized and winced. From their shoebox
My Barbies blubbered—but clemency had gone up
Like a tree line, so I buttered them. Salved their naked aches.

Prescribed amnesia and latitude. Meanwhile, a sister tripped
Trying to pilot the rupture. Another swept embers
Fat as macaws. The house wept tallow,

Soldered a fork in the road. The chimney settled
And swung ajar. And I, like Abednego, went on rendering
Flesh of my flesh, bone of my bone.

New Math

The sound of shoes fell away like a deck of cards
Let go one face at a time. Red minutes
In the laces, tongues

Like two versions of the same trapdoor. Along my fingertips,
Anxious fish. Heat chirping through the plural
Bones. Wasn't it awful,

The way I was suddenly laughing, then, my Popsicle mouth
Stuck like that? No matter how ample or empty
The house, you can always find

Slaphappy and stricken at the same table, sharing a wet bit of bread.
The school nurse said as much while my cot
Squawked and sagged.

Your arm's not broken. You'd be hollering if it were.
But she was wrong. I had cracked. Very.
Had dropped

Hard some necessary thing out by the backstop where we traded
Marbles: cat's-eyes, steelies, moss-blue boulders.
It's still there,

Damp and mangled as a mitten in the rain, as tonsils swamped
In your average longing. It's a little like the new math
How this can happen.

A little like saying what you most need while some dear one
Can yet (though turned, though stepping sideways,
Whistling zero)

Hear. A little like history kissing geography kissing the remaindered
Soul the way you can raise up anyway
And say it again.

Pacific

Who can bear this surface: blooming
Romeo, dizzy henchman, barnyard
Of blight and sheen?

Tomorrow offers tulips
And a tourniquet. Yesterday's dressed
In bleeding wires we call *sunset*.

Today is soup, cross and unknowable
As the sea where a boat bobs
Hangdog. Or is that paper? A plank walk
Albatrossed with clouds?

You ask for happiness and the foghorn says *No*
And *No* again, stuck on it,
The way the beach is stuck on gulls
And reduction.

Better to be ratless, ransacked,
Ruined as a drowned doubloon. Better
To fall utterly, perfectly—fast and much.

Perhaps true bottom is that mythical Pacific,
Boneless as a baby. Perhaps new eyes can be limned
For its particulars, lungs dispensed with
Like suffering.

Up here, the sky is full of water, the wind
Is full of sand. Our ears are full of fog
And the fretting lighthouse.

Just now it's calling out something
About danger and something about home.
We can nearly decipher both.

Heaven

Pigeons are not clean, not glorious, not still.
They shit on stained glass, on tire irons,

Their own blue claws. Each wing beat sends mites
And dust, feathers so slight we see them only

In the microscope of March light through barn slats,
Light that builds a table to show us what we breathe.

Nothing ever really settles. The axe handle buried
In rancid alfalfa ossifies to become your father's femur.

Burlap and mouse carcass twist into a ship that eats its own
Sails. You know only this: your seven-year-old self

Hasn't stopped swinging along the rungs of your ribcage.
And this: it will never be enough, the love

You were granted. Our voices move like sickles,
Our hands open to want. We stir. We rake the air

Into lavender ruin. Our barns will come down.

The Bath

after Bonnard's *Nu dans le bain au petit chein*

Let the letters come or not.
Let love find the drain or my far ear.
I'm renaming myself *Occupant.*
I'm swimming, elbow to porcelain,
In water cooled to the temperature
Of skin, in skin a little like spilled milk,
A little like caulk in the creases.

At first I was thinking rebuttal,
Retort; my body a "gone fishing" sign.
But somewhere I lost motive, lost
The monophony of *You'll be sorry*
And found the tub suited me at soul-level.
Its amniotic puckering. Its hard crown
Like a caul portending wearable rain;
Portending sorrow turned hydraulic:
Pipe and flute.

At first, the only music was slipshod:
Wind along the pane, afternoon picking
The lock to lie on the rug, nose to tail.
Now I hear broader, faster. There are pings
And sighings, harpful noises siphoned
From beyond the blonde enamel, beyond
My own pining which once seemed
Oceanic, a whale of a world—all mouth,
No ribs, no pity.

Maybe it's all this submersion.
My thoughts have grown mossy. I'll admit
I've forgotten his name, the one that had me
Hardly breathing. I'll admit I've misplaced
The wants that sent me spinning
Below the surface I see only
Through a pinhole now,
Squinting.

Perfect Vertigo

Don't believe what you read—
The odds are no odder than before.
A sky drops snow and fiasco.

The light is bent and tin-can empty.
Jugglers man the sad trees, heaving lemons
And a litany of your missteps.

Duck.
Here they come over the parapets,
· Under your manacle of lisps and humps.

Over the overthrown ministry of histrionics.
Under your busted compass,
Your errancy, your featherless heart.

You know what they say: *Breathe*—as if
You weren't spit into the world
With that jewel in your throat. That sun.

Apple. Ache. Show them how well you can choke,
Then. How much you can swallow choking.
How little you can startle falling

In your beautifully torn shoes.
Pitch and jangle. Spill and veer,
Dear. Stumble, gorgeous.

II. Bestiary

First Fish

Like the lake, I am a cave on its back,
Belly divining the idea of afternoon,

Each organ pandering to the smell of light,
The milky lens that insists on *between*.

There is water and the fish-eye-green underside of lilies,
And then a bias of blue refracting a thousand

Partial dragonflies. It's anyone's guess
How far a body can rise, how much bending the world

Might do to further a transom from here—this troughed mirror—
To humidity's pocket: skinless, aspirant.

Wriggling through wing-light, tree-light, cloud-light,
Some clearing might endeavor to make a church of me,

Or bluebird or sundial. Revise my name, revise the mist
Lodged in my gills like an argument, but all fish

Are older than their names. It's anyone's guess
When time began to migrate leaving some of us in tar,

Some of us partially footed or frogged in the base of a tree.
Before the sun became an animal, before the phyla

Of stars pecked *through,* we were alone
With the notion of loneliness. We moved through it

Like oldest water, trousseau of first things.

Fiji Mermaid

1.

She was filmy as a minnow, our girl—
A newt, permeable as the mind.
She waited by the trumpet creeper for a sign,
Hummed her fingers into bees,
Her feet above dissolve.

When she was starved for magic—and some are,
Some are born this way—a stranger gifted her an egg,
A shoot of bamboo, jam in a white dish,
And there was magic: out of a hat,
A net, a floppy shoe. Out of a sack of sugar.

There was no clear circus, so she tightroped
Breakfast, breathing, the buzzing wires
Stretched between any two human poles.
Wonder needed inventing; much did.

There were summers hewn by dragonflies,
Hillocks, river places, stammering horizons.
There was something sad in the water.
When morning came, she heard plaintive
Grasses, the heart-tones of doves in the eaves.
She kissed her own knees.

2.

Some are born two-headed, hatchling, full of crumbs.
Some are made this way, by which I mean
Unmade: the once-self pierced messily,
Gnawed through like rope or mercy, refashioned
To fall with the greatest of ease.

Upland from the upended manger of the body,
The soul builds its sodden nest. If I had one thing
To say to my god, that flawed father,
It might be *Why?* Might be, *Come nearer.*

Kissing Bug

We called it and it came: red-edged, eyeless,
the legs like filaments, antennae like black thread
we might tug on to loose the yard from its itchy skirt,
the cul-de-sac from six pink streetlights.

Several blocks away, a transistor hissed our back story.
Someone was leaving on a jet plane. Someone sang
baby baby baby until it was a bridge pulsed into place.
We considered jumping in order to fly.
We considered the tadpole evening and sighed.

In truth, the kissing bug didn't kiss, it bit the blue skin
around a knee, the lobe of a lightly furred ear.
This didn't hurt so much as startle us and later,
we would see an anthill, hardly red at all,
where the bug had not kissed.

There were lace-winged songs coming
from years away. We collected them and watched
for a skin to form. We kissed nothing. Not each other,
not ourselves, and this kick-started a kind of low-grade fever—
viral, ventral. We wore it deep and quiet.

At twilight, we pushed grass cuttings into long lanes
and raced the baby frogs there. The frogs peed on our hands,
lunged into the frog-colored grass, made noises
we couldn't hear. There were long star-addled evenings.
There was a kissing-bug kind of love everywhere we looked.

You and me: we made a noise no one heard. Our skin
became that noise. Feverful. Lostful. Truth:
the frogs panicked in our hands. Panicking, they sang.
Singing, they raced without meaning to toward the end
of the improbable lane.

Two-Headed Nightingale

Christine and Millie, conjoined twins born in North Carolina, 1851

1.

My sister begins at my sacrum, ends
at the down of my pillow with a cough. Listen to her—
wrist creak, spine sigh, canticle of quieter marrow.

I make music too: strum the wintered wall,
pluck a smoking candle, strain toward
unseeable treetops where magpies chide,
unbuilding the sky.

2.

My sister begins. She is ligature,
bellwether, carillon, lamp.

Behind me, she vines in sleep. Does not turn
but *is* a turn (curl, cup)—sacrament
of difficult bones. The benefactress
of all my hurting.

3.

Mother says that from the beginning
we wriggled away from her hands and nearer
each other, pressing and pliant. She knit us
a scalloped gown with two collars,
the skirt belled to swallow
four kicking legs.

When it was clear we'd live,
she traced our outline on wax paper.
Something of a valentine we were.
One bird: two tongues: a body and a second
same body—kissing, worried. Wed.

4.

I feel more than see her.

5.

I feel her *more*.

6.

Where I go to dream, it's snowing. There are things
to climb: cloud ledges, tabernacles.
Sometimes I let go the burden of her breathing,
her heavy goodness, the way she won't stop
saving me.

Sometimes I fall singing into the well
of my own contralto. Dusky bucket. Dense,
evident woods I might breach to free
a zero hour, fledgling vibrations,
my peeled self.

7.

I was born stuck. I was born bordered
and spared. Spooned away from bedlam,
from tumbledown, from blissful
discord.

I was born twice and if I am ever to become
unborn, it must be twice as well.
A severing and a severing.

8.

One bird—but cleft—the way a mind is.
The way the moon is—now bright and uncauterized.
Now tannic. Now forgiven.

I love her like my own tongue, my sister.
I wish she'd die.

9.

Others find us fashionably queer.
We've sung for a queen, jumped silk rope
in lavish salons, Virginia-reeled with twins.

We've hatched plans for a double wedding
while dawn hissed and puddled and refused
to show the future as anything
but minor cord and sideshow.

10.

We braid hands under the coverlet.

11.

My sister sings. Each satin note is suture:
exquisite, everywhere. Morning begins this way, and dreams.
And death, I think—half hymn, half harness
pinning wings.

Platypus, Dreaming

The platypus dreams eight hours a day.
—Scientific American

If I'm hungry, it's because I've been dreaming
among stones, wrestling with a mother's terror—

my unborn forced through aperture into fable,
eggs rinsed blue, too soft, dissolving
as I nudge them. These nightmares assure me

I have much to say about love. Everything's about love
and morning solves nothing. I dream through it

as through a door, drawing on the same eight notes,
the roe of a creature fabulous as myself: part bird,
part bruise, part dark looking when the lights go out.

Here, the dreams say. *Hear,* say the unclenched echoes.

If I'm tired, it's because I've been listening
the way night does, curling itself around the smallest
whimper—and yet nothing is spelled or sheer.

Nothing is nearer. If I've become lost,

it's because the algae has been dreamed into dragonfly.
Sediment into mirror. Nest into elegy.

Dreaming makes me and makes the world over again,
piecemeal. Gauzy stars are drawn down and quartered.
The high bank is resketched as eddy, and I am cast

as light in my first memory of waking. If I am suddenly
happy, it's because I'm awake now.

There is something like sun on the water.

Jersey Devil

Broken bell, cloud rent, curdled cry:
I mean to wake you. Wrest your safe
sighing. Jimmy the locks. Lob a startle
into the bunker of your light sleep,
the bed I spend much of my time
imagining. *How wide? How stained?*
How strewn with children yawning?
Children turning? Children whole?

Shall I tell you how I found *my* first bed?
The wet leaves my face fought
for a parcel of breath? The webs
in my lashes. The dirt I nursed from
and the pebbles for making teeth?
I loved my fingers. Fleshy pads
like florets, perfect for learning seed
and larvae, wild red of berries. The nails
for scratching *self* in a cradle of roots,
other in smoke and stone, *always*
in the sky unskeining.

I loved my fingers until I found my voice.
I wept to hear myself—throttled,
at first, and cottony—then a canyon
blooming, bruised. Rabbits scattered
at my ratcheting and black-souled crows.
Feral cats skulked into reedy evening.
Stars flinched.

Call me *devil* but I have seen my form.
The scaly folds boned for flapping.
The pit of tenderness that is my left eye.
I'm something purer. I'm good for small
spaces and for howling. I'm good
for stuffing memory back behind the pines
where I see you stooping, still bloody
along the thighs, to deposit me sleeping.
No pardon. No passional, wasteful
weeping. No charm to ward off
the clawed, awful things near the river
and in my head.

The river is a sibling now. It slakes me
and takes my singing for its own. I sing.
I save my fattest notes for you, posting them
on the chance swing of wind, seeking your ear,
caulked behind fences and pillars, as it is, behind
darlings in the yard, playing at blindness.

Come night, I watch the moon starve
and shadows inhabit the pocket. I watch water
twitch, retreating, and coppery fish quicken
to fill the vacuum until I understand ebb
and echo and collapse, how the sky is a sponge
for my lowing, how damp grasses bow and part.
Come sleep, I am loud, Mother—louder.
When you left off dreaming about me, I became
no less a thing in a dream. No less divine.

Sloth, Swimming

for Lisa

When she fell she flapped and dragged
At vines and went on falling,

Her splash buckling reeds,
Drowning leaves foamed with frogs' eggs.

Everything needed swimming—rocks, then silt
Then thick water. There were new sounds—

They didn't belong to her—and a pain
That did. It moved with her

Through a scrim of thrashing damselflies.
Perhaps she was dying.

Perhaps this was death—eucalyptus
Forever behind her in the canopy, eucalyptus

With its clustered berries, its resin settling
Like memory into the trunk's lung.

And her lungs, what were they up to?
What was the world up to now that she could only

Steep in it, swallowing deeply? Her mind
Was above the current for now, but soon everything

Would be translated into the fish word for *water*.
She could feel the word against her belly fur.

It was with her—water—it had come between.
She would never know why.

Jackalope

Something must have mothered me,
Rare as I am, shy of light as I am.

When evening comes—purple cleft and plow,
Stain of night birds, shadow trees hobbling

The far rise—I come looking for my own kind,
Looking for you, jackalope. They say

You're stitched from two sad animals,
That you're mongrel and luminous,

That your sob is so tuneful, so human
It makes cowboys buckle and kneel.

Makes desert flowers strain from their centers.
And when the fire dies. When night is all cargo,

Barrow and badland, you come nearer,
Queer and quiet, smelling fear on me

Everlasting. You know me as you know
Outlaw ballads, the runaway moon.

There is only one loneliness. We share it
As we share a sky, the fable of forgetting,

A clamor, a cry.

Snow Fence

How is it my Yeti belongs to me?
Like yours he is leviathan and loud
With snow. Like yours, reluctant to forgive
Tears and trespasses, to spell his name
Into a palm damp with expectation.

I promised to be satisfied with the blind meadow,
Blizzards of whitish needles, wind
Manifest along ascending ridges. But night
Is never far from us, and with it, rumblings
Of attachment in the larger belly.

I thought to whisper only. Thought to love
Generally, the way snow loves.
But now, something is avalanching.
Perhaps it is the monster throwing off
My claim to him. Perhaps a sigh

Fisting over itself like a barrel toward the living.
Or one body forgetting everything
But momentum. Below, our village cowers—
Pallor of bells, icicles trembled thinner,
Children herding their own cries with fat mittens.

At our blunted edge: drifts, a bridge
Distilled from ice floe, the hammered
Pickets of a snow fence. See how its shadow
Builds a second, grayer cage. See how like
Soul it is, and all the beautiful weight behind.

III. Peace in the Valley

Genesis

The early earth was hollow—empty
dress form—wire monkey
newborns clung to not knowing
any better. So it is with hunger,

with beginnings. Day pecked a radius,
collared the sea monsters off to one side
where they seethed, boiled, went temporarily mute.
Tomato vines belly-crawled, binding

the foal to its melancholy, the goose
to its lumbering, the moon to its brilliant skewer.
All of this was practice. A fluke punch
landing solid, and there we were with our new fur,

our allotment: serpents, fig dust,
sprung rain—and that pendulum
memory, lunging back like an angel on a tear.
So it is with suffering,

with inheritance. Lark and swale and rucksack;
the halt and the toppled; the rapt
and the prodigal—a snarl of oddments
each according to its kind. Flushed,
breathing, making do.

Late Garden

Seven fruit trees and a red wagon.
Water sloshing in five-gallon buckets.

> *I remember you,*
> *perhaps you exist.*

One road unpaved, wilting sawgrass,
weather barbing like fence line.

> *The worst that can happen*
> *has already happened.*

When the pump arm squawks, a tune rises
in the mouth like shell casing, fruit pit,
something scorched.

> *We're fashioned to endure,*
> *I will endure you.*

Up the hill and back, wearing the obvious groove.
And then, perhaps, in June:
a nectarine.

Woman, Counting

One

Ellipses chewed like frozen peas, she counts herself
back. Lawns and fathers are reversible.
Summer is a mute liquid she flails through,
swimming suit tight, ears filling, sinking, cast away.

> *There, at the birth of a line*
> *turned endwise to the eye*

The kingdom of memory uncastled is sand,
small and several. She counts grains, just the ones she can see
to grieve for. She counts the holes other creatures make vanishing;
patinaed starfish; daubs of pink decomposing
in the purloined sky.

Two

In a cereal box: a click-toy with trigger
and numbered wheel meant for counting train cars or crows
on a wire. Or the times a sister kicked her surreptitiously.
Or the miscellany of sorrows that dreamed their way
onto her lap.

Before this, there were her fingers and toes to consider,
hills and stars and fruit trees—all of which woke her
with their loud breathing.

> *glad avenue, bit of string*

There were lemon-colored ditches sucking on themselves,
roads that bellied out and went black.
Sometimes, she felt she was on the brink of something.
That something was on the brink of her.

Three

The kingdom of memory is the kingdom of counting
on nothing but mosquitoes and saltines.
Bald tires. Hot feet. Gas station candy.

I follow her

She starts backwards from a hundred or sometimes simply
from where she is, stopping to knock on the door
of each year to see who might answer.

Eight runs the water in the bathroom all night,
pencils coins over the eyes of her quiet cotton bear.
Thirteen is sunburned, sleeping in a corner chair,
sidling up to Jesus saying, "It's enough now, isn't it?"

Four

The kingdom of memory is a plastic-wrapped cup
that will hear anything she might sob into it,
never empty, never full.

counting pale days, as in winter

Decades crest and growl like bodies of water. She counts
hotel keys, fire doors, nests of wet washcloths—
naming them with numbers.

Turning to a darkened window,
she regards her body, which, after each slow division,
is somehow hers to give.

pale nights, as in Now that you
are gone
my eyes have become my
hands.

The Wrong Monster

"The monster is better when it startles us"
—Robert Pinsky

Once there were black shadows. They owned
Every crevice, their black hands perfect for this.
Once a tree branch tortured the moorings,
But it's frighteningly quiet now.

Something snuck in and hit the lights.
Now they're always on. The door won't slam.
The wind is soft as butter, guttural. My neighbors
Are forever awake—I hear them dancing—
Accordions and a mandolin, their loud, real feet.

Look closely at this house I built with worry.
Chewed paper for the walls, stripped quills
For the roof and ribs. How is it nothing falls
Now, nothing burns?

How is it my wet lungs work, in and out
And in again as the lover—who doesn't leave,
Who keeps not leaving—turns toward me, says,
You've had a bad dream. Says, Tell me.

Blue Circus

Limping with, muddied with, raw with blue
comes our circus—comes blowsy,
comes stunted, comes crumbs.

Shall we keep it? Stake a broad tent in the field
pocked by asteroids? Rig cages for the things
that will moan there? Fashion tightropes
and hoops, the blue ribs of nooses?

You and I—we're awake now on this gradient slope,
though we cannot fathom how this came to be,
how in another ring—tucked up near the denser organs—
our lungs glow like drowned lanterns, our hearts
climb an impossible ladder, lunge
toward the vanishing pool.

Real Time

Another letter spoken late
Into a drain in a stranger's house
Which could be my body.

This last letter and no more sound
About the troubling knots that catch at the teeth
When I say, *Love me.*

Cramp of memory. Bedlam in the joints
And joists. Boomerang soul
Like a cowboy bullet in the graveyard.

Was I born this impatient, this wrought
With small stairs and banisters?

I turn cards, consult apple cores, beg names
From the milk dried to filigree in my saucer.

Of the sidewalk cracks and the interstitial
Weeds. Of the curb's coarse lip
And my sternum, I ask only *When?*

When they bother to answer
It is with blooming—the slowest possible give—

And I hear my hooded blood as backup singer
Full of shimmy and mystery:
You are here.

That's her line and again with a roll
Of the shoulders and a snap of tambourine
Fingers and an X and an O

And an *Oh* sighed from dead center.

Proof

I was born lost to myself in a thin litter,
Jostling the bodies to each side for milk

And a soul. No wonder I crouch now in the easy
Province of other animals—over stolen fire, red bone

Of morning, the cloverleaf of a print headed away.
Everywhere there is proof of their happiness.

I drop to the path, finger the leaf bed impressed
With a congress of small close forms. Still warm.

Perennial

The past is female—feminine
Unending, unremitting, unresolved—

Like a letter stuck in vague address:
Dear _____ crowding the date.

Dear _____ like a herd of one
Nosing seedlings under snow.

*

In one myth of my girlhood, the baby
Wore doll's clothes, dotted-Swiss collar
Pinned to a pillowcase to keep her
From slipping away. In another, her faith
Was miniature—a hank of cotton
Seeded with small noises.

Sometimes there was water nearby,
Sometimes a dense thicket or a path
Forking toward a smoke-colored house.
Behind her, lost things traveled
In bulb form, kicking their way
Slowly round.

*

The past is female and its shadow also,
And the place it finds to lie down,
Curled a little on its side, female too.

I like to think of it as the egg of the *I*
Buried under lightly tilled soil.
I like to think I'm tending that egg.
Here, now, tending it. Or loving it, rather.

The Next Good Thing

Magpies are one kind of noise here, one
kind of persistence, mess, marvel. Plain grasses grate
and wheeze. A black snake sleeps like rope
near the cattle guard. Ants castle the borders,
leach sand in a collective mouth.

Somehow, you haven't spent everything, not yet—
haven't bet, haven't lost too much to lean and crest
the ridge where you have come to meet
the next good thing.

This is the West you came for, pocked with prairie dogs,
red in unlikely places. Weeds splinter piecemeal
in a buckshot wind. The knuckle of your heart
rattles awake. Your shoes patina,
press coins into the road.

Milk

This was no motel-time, borrowed pillow
Like a dime between the knees, the TV's mosquito
Stitching my open ear with policies of loss.

Well above the road too like pulled string,
The train weeping smoke, I traveled in milk. Held. Substantial.
The slow eye of a sustainable bloom.

As I slept, a shore pulsed nearer: lover's hip
Or the heart pledging more to the body than the fist
Of its function. On the third day, I woke

To find myself blown like seed-fluff over a nation
Of grazing animals. Become: a silo's satellite. Barn's moon.
I counted towns like lost shoes and soon was less

A wife and more like Nebraska. This can happen
In the Midwest, the labor of fields thrown down like a broad,
Bright sieve and a life pressed through.

Ark

If my story is paper, so is yours—
single sheet folded variously, damp
in the creases, perishable as sleep.

We are most ourselves when, in a vast,
troubled dream, we glimpse that vessel
which will bear us further on,
your several animals and mine

braying plainly. Our fathers nestled in the hold
like casks of brine, our mothers in the crow's nest,
spooning up unsettled doves.

Whatever is hungriest will topple us,
tug us down to where mountains tread water,
where any covenant can become
a slight, blind fish lost to itself.

How could we not know this?
How could we not love anyway?

.

Peace in the Valley

There was a hole with a hole in it.
This was my valley—amply yellow.
Bowed as broom straw.

Daily it rested in the hollow
That described it. Stripped hills rose around
And the world around that, and then a fabric

Starred with memorial, expressly distant.
Whatever the weather, whatever grief
Accrued in the sloughs and gullies,

Below stayed below. Borders sagged
And refused to signify. Birds
Learned to imagine an elsewhere.

What did not fly in my valley included children
And stones. Rough varieties and calico,
And those still wishing to be carried.

There were no tears, as each animal had cried
Itself out early on. So, yes, quiet
Where the weeping had been. A barrow of salt

Where the sea had been. And a hole, winnowed,
Crenellated, where the body sheltered once,
And slept.

Mudbaby

Four doves on a rooftop, heads pressed
Into a kind of grief knot,

Tail feathers askew as the mind's compass.
Winter has made a sign of us all,

Even the squirrel my son has named Martin,
Who picks through our yard

As if pacing off the lengths of a treasure map.
He won't find a third of what he's buried,

Nor will I. It's February. My belly thickens
Around beginnings. I'm tender

And unbalanced, baffled as something newly
Excavated. Come spring, as the story goes,

I will increase, contriving soul enough for two.
Who would believe any of this,

How the mudbaby left in a field for the crows
To mother becomes a mother herself,

And more than this, becomes happy
In the mudhouse of her body?

Who would believe the world, abandoned
To her own will—manifold, pilgrimmed

Spinning—would dig us all out of the dark?

Notes

"Enough with the Angels" is for Alice Fulton.

"Heaven" (page 12) is for James and Erika Airheart.

"Acrobats with Oranges" is after Renoir's painting *Acrobats at the Circus Fernando.*

The reference to Shadrack, Meshack and Abednego in "Old Testament" refers to the account in Daniel 3:19–23 of three young Hebrew men who, refusing to bow down to the image in gold of King Nebuchadnezzar, are thrown into a fiery furnace but do not perish.

"Heaven" (page 16) is for Harry Bauld.

The Fiji (or Feejee) Mermaid is widely considered to be one of the biggest hoaxes in circus history. It is said that P.T. Barnum purchased the creature from a fisherman who had stitched together the bodies of a baby orangutan and a fish, and the head of a monkey. In order to boost public curiosity as well as "authenticate" the creature, Barnum enlisted the help of a friend to pose as one Dr. Griffen, an English gentleman/scientist who arrived in New York in 1842 bearing a spectacular find, a real mermaid he claimed was caught near the Fiji Islands. He was reportedly on his way to England where the mermaid was to become part of the collection of the Lyceum of Natural History. However, because of considerable interest in the creature, Dr. Griffin agreed to exhibit it for a week with other "hybrid species" such as the duckbill platypus and flying fish. Afterwards, the mermaid was moved to the American Museum, which had recently come under the ownership of P.T. Barnum. The Mermaid went on to become one of Barnum's longest running and most popular attractions—drawing a profit of some one thousand dollars a week. Currently, there are said to be seven Fiji Mermaids on display in America.

"Kissing Bug" is for Katherine Sullivan Baldock.

"Two-Headed Nightingale": Conjoined twins Millie and Christine McKay (McKoy or McCoy in some sources) were connected at the base of the spine. Born into slavery in North Carolina in 1851, they were sold and displayed as freak show performers. Billed as the "Two-headed Nightingale," or the "Two-headed Woman," they toured the United States and Europe singing duets and accompanying themselves on the keyboard. Before returning to America, where their career continued with much success, the sisters met Queen Victoria, who thought them "charming and unusual." Christine was the stronger of the pair and could lift Millie off the ground simply by leaning forward. Millie succumbed to tuberculosis on October 12, 1912, and Christine followed 17 hours later. They were 61 years of age, making them the oldest living female conjoined twins.

The jackalope—a species of antlered rabbit—is a creature of American folklore. In the old West, when cowboys would gather around campfires to sing, jackalopes were said to be heard singing back, mimicking human voices. Douglas, Wyoming has declared itself the jackalope capital of America because, according to legend, the first jackalope was spotted there in 1829. An enormous statue of the jackalope stands in the town center. Douglas Herrick, a long-time resident of Douglas, Wyoming, is often credited with the popularization of the jackalope. In the 1930s, he and his brother Ralph began mounting and selling jackalope heads to the public—these and postcards of the creatures became popular Western souvenirs.

The Jersey Devil is a beast with the head of a horse, large wings and claws and an approximately four-foot-long serpentine body. Although there are many stories as to its origins, spanning back some 260 years, one of the most common is this: In 18th century New Jersey, a woman named Mother Leeds, living in poverty with 12 children, found out she was to have another child. In despair she cursed the unborn child, saying, "Let it be a devil." When the child was born, it was horribly deformed. Some versions of the story say the monster-child crawled from the womb, flew up the chimney and into the woods where it still preys on livestock and small children. In other versions, Mother Leeds took the creature into the pine barrens and abandoned it there, where it can still be heard howling for her and for its own fate.

"Snow Fence" is after Wislawa Szymborska's poem, "Notes from a Nonexistent Himalayan Expedition," from *Calling out to Yeti,* 1957.

"Woman, Counting" began with thinking about the question, "Is not distance a line turned endwise to the eye?" from "Three Dialogues between Hilas and Philonius, in Opposition to Skeptics and Atheists," George Berkeley, 1713.

Epigraphs on these pages are attributed to the following sources:

Page 6: Blaise Pascal, *Thoughts.* Trans. WF Trotter. Cambridge: Harvard Classics, 1909–14.

Page 32: Thomas A. Dorsey, "Peace in the Valley," 1937.

Page 43: Robert Pinsky, "Lament for the Makers," *The Want Bone.* Hopewell: The Ecco Press, 1990.

Acknowledgements

Versions of these poems first appeared in:

The Antioch Review: "Perfect Vertigo"

The Black Warrior Review: "Heaven" (page 12)

The Gettysburg Review: "Enough with the Angels," "Milk," "New Math"

For their generous support and the gift of time, I would like to thank The National Endowment for the Arts, the Corporation of Yaddo, and the Ucross Foundation.

Thanks as well to my colleagues and students at New England College, to Herb Scott, for continued faith, to Glori Simmons for abiding friendship and good council, to Connor McLain Berglund for his early and enduring love of monsters, and to Greg D'Alessio, without whom this book would not exist.

Paula McLain received her MFA in poetry from the University of Michigan in 1996. Since then, she has been a work-study scholar at Bread Loaf Writer's Conference, a resident at Yaddo, the MacDowell Colony, and the Ucross Foundation, and a recipient of a fellowship from the National Endowment for the Arts. Her first book of poetry, *Less of Her,* was published in 1999 by New Issues Press and won a publication grant from the Greenwall Fund of the Academy of American Poets. Individual poems have appeared in numerous literary journals and in the anthology *American Poetry: The Next Generation.* Little, Brown and Co. published her memoir, *Like Family: Growing Up In Other People's Houses,* in 2003. She teaches in the low-residency program in poetry at New England College, and lives in Ohio.

New Issues Poetry & Prose

Editor, Herbert Scott

Gail Martin, *The Hourglass Heart*
David Marlatt, *A Hog Slaughtering Woman*
Louise Mathias, *Lark Apprentice*
Gretchen Mattox, *Buddha Box, Goodnight Architecture*
Paula McLain, *Less of Her; Stumble, Gorgeous*
Lydia Melvin, *South of Here*
Sarah Messer, *Bandit Letters*
Malena Mörling, *Ocean Avenue*
Julie Moulds, *The Woman with a Cubed Head*
Gerald Murnane, *The Plains* (fiction)
Marsha de la O, *Black Hope*
C. Mikal Oness, *Water Becomes Bone*
Bradley Paul, *The Obvious*
Elizabeth Powell, *The Republic of Self*
Margaret Rabb, *Granite Dives*
Rebecca Reynolds, *Daughter of the Hangnail, The Bovine Two-Step*
Martha Rhodes, *Perfect Disappearance*
Beth Roberts, *Brief Moral History in Blue*
John Rybicki, *Traveling at High Speeds* (expanded second edition)
Mary Ann Samyn, *Inside the Yellow Dress, Purr*
Ever Saskya, *The Porch is a Journey Different From the House*
Mark Scott, *Tactile Values*
Hugh Seidman, *Somebody Stand Up and Sing*
Martha Serpas, *Côte Blanche*
Diane Seuss-Brakeman, *It Blows You Hollow*
Elaine Sexton, *Sleuth*
Marc Sheehan, *Greatest Hits*
Sarah Jane Smith, *No Thanks—and Other Stories* (fiction)
Heidi Lynn Staples, *Guess Can Gallop*
Phillip Sterling, *Mutual Shores*
Angela Sorby, *Distance Learning*
Matthew Thorburn, *Subject to Change*
Russell Thorburn, *Approximate Desire*
Rodney Torreson, *A Breathable Light*
Robert VanderMolen, *Breath*
Martin Walls, *Small Human Detail in Care of National Trust*
Patricia Jabbeh Wesley, *Before the Palm Could Bloom: Poems of Africa*